Community Workers

Garbage Collectors

by Amy McDonald

BELLWETHER MEDIA
MINNEAPOLIS, MN

Blastoff! Beginners are developed by literacy experts and educators to meet the needs of early readers. These engaging informational texts support young children as they begin reading about their world. Through simple language and high frequency words paired with crisp, colorful photos, Blastoff! Beginners launch young readers into the universe of independent reading.

Sight Words in This Book

a	have	ride	they
and	into	some	to
at	is	the	
away	it	their	
day	on	these	

This edition first published in 2025 by Bellwether Media, Inc.

Library of Congress Cataloging-in-Publication Data

LC record for Garbage Collectors available at: https://lccn.loc.gov/2024038070

Editor: Betsy Rathburn   Designer: Laura Sowers

Printed in the United States of America, North Mankato, MN.

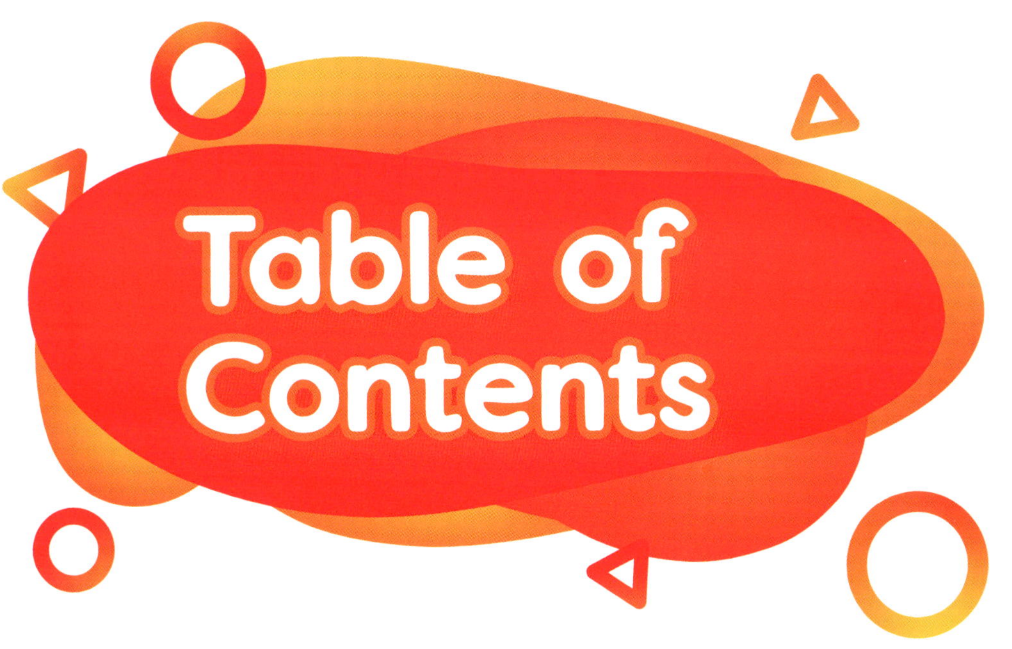

Table of Contents

On the Job

The bin is full!
It is trash day.

bin

80
90

What Are They?

Garbage collectors take away trash. They keep places clean.

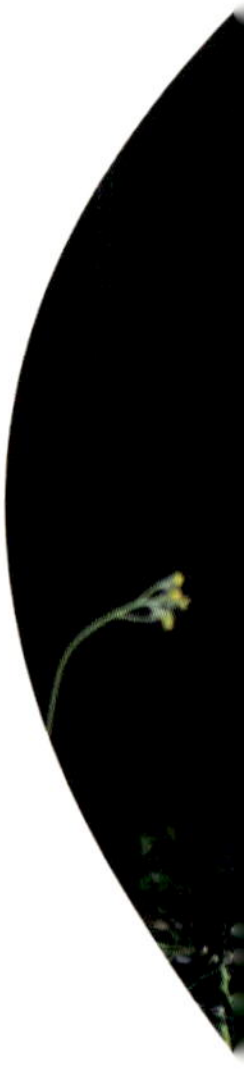

They drive around cities and towns.

MACK
ALLIED WASTE SERVICES

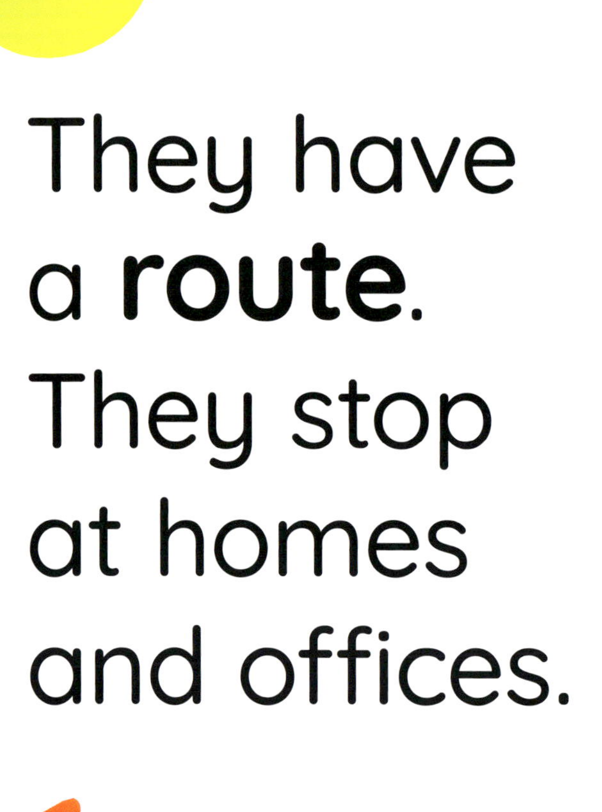

They have a **route**. They stop at homes and offices.

164
NE PAS

What Do They Do?

These workers have trucks. Some ride on the back.

They dump bins into the trucks.

They have
safety **gear**.
They wear gloves
and vests.

glove
vest

They drive to **landfills**. They drop off their **loads**.

load

Why Do We Need Them?

These workers take away trash. They work hard!

Garbage Collector Facts

Tools

truck

vest

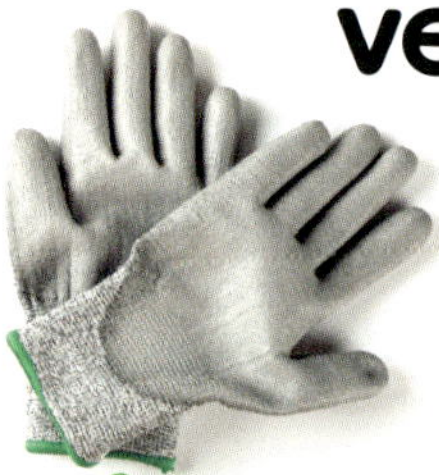

gloves

A Day in the Life

drive a truck

dump bins

drop off loads

Glossary

gear

special clothing

landfills

places where trash is dumped

loads

things carried by garbage trucks

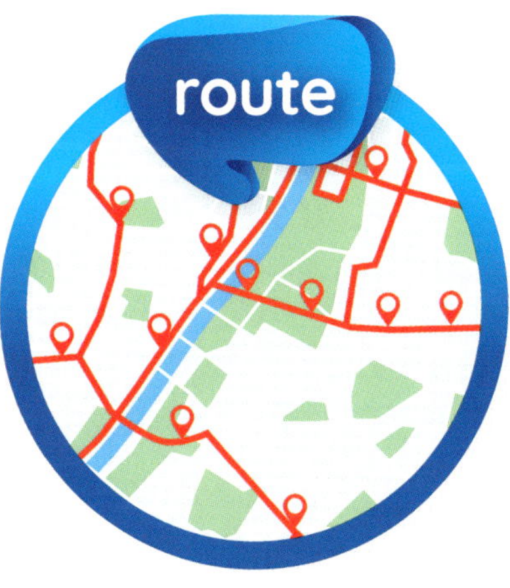

route

a path from one place to another

To Learn More

ON THE WEB

FACTSURFER

Factsurfer.com gives you a safe, fun way to find more information.

1. Go to www.factsurfer.com.
2. Enter "garbage collectors" into the search box and click 🔍.
3. Select your book cover to see a list of related content.

Index

The images in this book are reproduced through the courtesy of: Andrey_Popov, front cover; DreamHomeStudio, p. 3; Stokkete, p. 4; Grey Zone, pp. 4-5; AndreyPopov, pp. 6-7, 20-21; Michael T Hartman, pp. 8-9; Obatala-photography, pp. 10-11; Oporty786, p. 12; Dmitry Kalinovsky, pp. 12-13; dpa picture alliance/ Alamy, pp. 14-15; Ljupco Smokovski, p. 16; M2020, pp. 16-17; Jenya Smyk, p. 18; picturesd, pp. 18-19; Another77, p. 22 (truck); New Africa, pp. 22 (vest), 23 (gear); Jr images, p. 22 (gloves); Kzenon, p. 22 (drive a truck); Sirisak_baokaew, p. 22 (dump bins); Simlinger, p. 22 (drop off loads); vchal, p. 23 (landfills); GOLFX, p. 23 (loads); Art Alex, p. 23 (route).